W9-BUA-350

WALKING ON SUNSHINE

WALKING ON SUNSHINE

52 SMALL STEPS TO HAPPINESS

RACHEL KELLY

With illustrations by Jonathan Pugh

ATRIA BOOKS

New York   London   Toronto   Sydney   New Delhi

ATRIA BOOKS
An Imprint of Simon & Schuster, Inc.
1230 Avenue of the Americas
New York, NY 10020

First Atria Books hardcover edition November 2016

ATRIA BOOKS and colophon are trademarks of Simon & Schuster, Inc.

For information about special discounts for bulk purchases, please contact Simon & Schuster Special Sales at 1-866-506-1949 or business@simonandschuster.com.

The Simon & Schuster Speakers Bureau can bring authors to your live event. For more information, or to book an event, contact the Simon & Schuster Speakers Bureau at 1-866-248-3049 or visit our website at www.simonspeakers.com.

Interior design by Georgia Vaux

Manufactured in the United States of America

10   9   8   7   6   5   4   3   2   1

Library of Congress Cataloging-in-Publication Data
Names: Kelly, Rachel (Journalist), author.
Title: Walking on sunshine : 52 small steps to happiness / by Rachel Kelly ;
   illustrations by Jonathan Pugh.
Description: First [edition]. | New York City : Atria Books, 2016. | Includes
   bibliographical references.
Identifiers: LCCN 2016017962 (print) | LCCN 2016037446 (ebook) | ISBN
   9781501146442 (hardcover) | ISBN 9781501146480 ()
Subjects: LCSH: Happiness--Miscellanea.
Classification: LCC BJ1481 .K37 2016 (print) | LCC BJ1481 (ebook) | DDC
   158.1--dc23
LC record available at https://lccn.loc.gov/2016017962

ISBN 978-1-5011-4644-2
ISBN 978-1-5011-4648-0 (ebook)

For my parents

Introduction . . . *x*

S P R I N G . . . *1*

1. The Spring Is Coming . . . 2

2. Turn Control into Curiosity . . . 4

3. A Helping Hand . . . 6

4. Mindful Moments . . . 8

5. Stuffocation . . . 10

6. Prayer . . . 12

7. Three-Step Breathing Exercise . . . 14

8. Unplug . . . 16

9. Embrace the New Day . . . 18

10. Think Positive . . . 20

11. Words You Say . . . 22

12. Habit Tacking . . . 24

13. Gratitude . . . 26

SUMMER . . . *29*

14. I Will Arise . . . 30

15. Fly on the Wall . . . 32

16. Learn to Love the Journey . . . 34

17. Find Exercise You Enjoy . . . 36

18. Reaching Out . . . 38

19. Balm of Hurt Minds . . . 40

20. Flower Power . . . 42

21. If You Can Keep Your Head . . . 44

22. Nourish Your Body . . . 46

23. The Sound of Running Water . . . 48

24. The Joy of Missing Out . . . 50

25. Mending . . . 52

26. Home Calmer Home . . . 54

AUTUMN . . . *57*

27. Make Me Thy Lyre . . . 58

28. Bird by Bird . . . 60

29. Make Mistakes . . . 62

30. Box Sets . . . 64

31. The Road Better Traveled . . . 66

32. Find a Companion . . . 68

33. Find Your Midpoint . . . 70

34. Body Language . . . 72

35. Wallow . . . 74

36. Unwind . . . 76

37. What You Resist Persists . . . 78

38. The Magic of Baking . . . 80

39. Formation Flying . . . 82

WINTER ... *85*

40. The Sky Is Low ... 86

41. Human Beings, Not Human Doings ... 88

42. Secret Breathing Exercise ... 90

43. HALT ... 92

44. Psychobiotics ... 94

45. Habit Releasing ... *96*

46. Alcohol ... *98*

47. Play ... 100

48. The 60 Percent Rule ... 102

49. Bottled Sunshine ... 104

50. Rainbow Foods ... 106

51. Meditation ... 108

52. Unhistoric Acts ... 110

Closing Thoughts: Whose Voices Are They Anyway? *112*

Acknowledgments *115*

Further Reading *116*

Notes to Self *118*

P.S. Falling off the Wagon ... *130*

INTRODUCTION

In this book I share what I've learned about staying calm and happy in a diary of my year. For me the two are intrinsically linked: I often feel joyful as a result of feeling calm.

Last year, I published a memoir entitled *Black Rainbow: How Words Healed Me—My Journey Through Depression* in which I describe my past experience of debilitating depression and how I recovered from this serious illness. The book was based on diary entries, letters, and emails that I wrote at the time.

Since then, I've continued to get better. I've also continued my habit of writing letters and keeping a diary. And this time, I've been able to move away from the heavy stuff and focus on what helps me through what Freud called "ordinary human unhappiness"—the inevitable ups and downs of everyday life rather than depression. Most days now, I feel steady and well—and sometimes I even feel as if I'm walking on sunshine.

I've experienced this newfound sense of well-being partly because I've been very lucky. When my memoir came out, I was fortunate to receive letters and emails from readers who were generous enough to share their own stories. I've since tried out many of their suggestions for leading a happier life, some of which are included here. Other ideas have come from giving talks and running workshops for mental health charities, schools, universities, and businesses.

The result is *Walking on Sunshine*, a collection of fifty-two small, sanity-saving tools that have worked for me and proved to be my friends throughout the year. All of them have served as shortcuts to happier, more conscious living.

In general, I've found that while these steps may not directly lead to happiness, it often follows as a by-product. Such is the paradoxical nature of happiness. You cannot simply become happy, like flicking a switch in your head. Rather happiness is often an indirect consequence of the way we think and our actions, whether it's tending a garden or helping others. I've also found that small steps work best. They are not only achievable but add up and have been the easiest way for me to make sustainable changes. I've found that every time I try a more dramatic approach, I set the bar too high and end up feeling a failure.

It's proved helpful to be aware of the particular pressures of different times of year. As a mother, I find there are challenges associated with the academic calendar. And Christmas in particular is a season that I've found needs a health warning on it. My state of mind is also affected by changes in weather and light.

The book is an eclectic mix, something of a salad bowl of ideas from which readers can pick and choose what works for them. To this end, there is space at the back of the book for you to write your own notes and reflections.

There are some thoughts on diet, bits on breathing, some philosophical nuggets, a spot of prayer and poetry, sayings that help me through, exercises that I practice, and a sprinkling of mindfulness. This ancient Buddhist approach to life incorporates meditation and breathing exercises and has particularly helped me slow down.

So too has a basic biology lesson, which I will share with you here. If you fail to relax, your body is forced to rely on backup energy courtesy of your adrenal system—a handy trick when running from a predator or chasing prey, but less than ideal as a strategy for everyday life.

Your adrenal system runs on adrenaline and cortisol. These are the fight-or-flight hormones that keep you in a constant state of high alert. Cortisol also inhibits your brain's uptake of the mood-elevating hormone serotonin, which makes you more prone to anxiety. We are designed to accommodate stress, but only in short bursts. That's why the frantic twenty-four-hour stress that so many of us live with today is so damaging.

I hope one or two of my steps may help you slow down and open doors to a place of greater happiness—and that you too may sometimes have that lovely feeling of walking on sunshine.

Rachel Kelly, London, September 2015

SPRING

MARCH ~ APRIL ~ MAY

1. THE SPRING IS COMING

We are just back from a family trip to the Lake District. Printed below is John Clare's "Young Lambs," his celebration of spring as a time of renewal, when all sorts of things seem possible. This poem slows me down and makes me appreciate and be more attentive to my surroundings, which I tend to ignore when I'm busy and overwhelmed.

The spring is coming by a many signs;
The trays are up, the hedges broken down,
That fenced the haystack, and the remnant shines
Like some old antique fragment weathered brown.
And where suns peep, in every sheltered place,
The little early buttercups unfold
A glittering star or two—till many trace
The edges of the blackthorn clumps in gold.
And then a little lamb bolts up behind
The hill and wags his tail to meet the yoe,
And then another, sheltered from the wind,
Lies all his length as dead—and lets me go
Close bye and never stirs but baking lies,
With legs stretched out as though he could not rise.

Clare describes the first signs of the unfolding season in loving detail. He sees "little early buttercups unfold" into "a glittering star or two." The haystacks from the last harvest have been dismantled and are ready for a new crop, leaving only a shining "remnant" of hay behind. These winter leftovers are so out of place they seem like "some old antique fragment" in a scene where everything else is renewed and brimming with possibility.

A lamb bounds out to meet the poet and "wags his tail." Another, basking in the sun, "with legs stretched out as though he couldn't rise," allows him to walk right up. Spring, to Clare, is best represented by a newborn animal, so carefree that it remains flat on its back, enjoying the sunshine even when the poet approaches. Stopping for a moment to imagine Clare's sunbathing lamb always makes me smile.

2 . T U R N   C O N T R O L   I N T O   C U R I O S I T Y

This March morning is ringing with promise. The skies are clear and the sun is bright. It's the sort of day that makes me want to straighten up the house and get the children to help. They are reluctant. Rather like Mole in *The Wind in the Willows*, their view is: "Hang spring-cleaning!"

I often use mantras to embed new ideas, and a favorite of mine in such circumstances is: "Turn control into curiosity."

Control is closely linked to anxiety. I usually try to tell others what to do as a response to feeling insecure myself, and, yes, ironically, out of control. And so now every time I find myself bossing around others, I ask myself why. I've found I'm typically imposing my own agenda on those around me and dictating how I feel the world should run, rather than receiving the world as it is.

The much more relaxing option may be to stop, breathe, and turn control into curiosity. Why, I wonder, do I want others to come and help me tidy up? What are my motives? The answer is that I'm feeling unsettled. I want to enforce a sense of order on my surroundings so I feel calmer on the inside.

When I am able to overcome the urge to control, and instead trust that things will work out the way they are meant to, I can begin to enjoy the moment more fully. My family will tidy up, albeit in half an hour's time. If someone challenges my assumptions, I can be curious rather than affronted. And there's something very liberating in that.

3 . A HELPING HAND

Today is my day to volunteer at the education department of a men's prison housed in a series of dilapidated redbrick Victorian buildings not far from our house. The work reflects whatever the education department requires. This morning we are concentrating on teaching the inmates interview skills for the prison magazine. On other occasions I've run poetry-writing workshops. Writing poems can be an outlet to help the men express difficult feelings. Unlikely as it sounds, writing love poetry is always the most popular option.

Our team of volunteers and prison staff gather in a room with about ten prisoners. The atmosphere is usually collaborative and uncompetitive, with a real sense of shared purpose, though sometimes the sessions are difficult and those who attend are unresponsive.

But even then the mood in the room may suddenly change when an inmate makes an emotional connection with the work in hand. These are magical moments that unite us. For that brief time, the poem is all there is. I forget any prison guards and the security training we had to undertake, in which it was made clear that we must be ever vigilant and aware that visitors are at risk of attack by the prisoners.

When feeling caught up in one's own worries, it can be difficult to try and engage with others. At times I feel I don't have an ounce of energy left over for anyone else. But overcoming this obstacle has proved a blessing. I always leave the prison with some new insight or having discovered a new writer. Some of the prisoners—often the older men—have heads richly stocked with poetry that they share with the group, enriching us all.

4. MINDFUL MOMENTS

I step out of a stressful meeting to wash my hands. On my return, my mood is much more mellow. Here's why.

One way to relieve tension is to incorporate a *mindful activity* into your busy day; I decided a few years ago that hand washing would be mine. You can choose your own: brushing your hair, cleaning your teeth, or some other routine activity that you would otherwise do unconsciously.

You can perform your activity whenever you feel frazzled to bring your mind back to the present moment. There's plenty of evidence that mindfulness can benefit people's lives, but those I've discussed it with usually say how hard it is to find the time to practice—thus the need to incorporate it into one's established patterns of behavior.

I consciously enjoy feeling the coldness of the water, hearing it splashing against the basin, smelling the soap's scent, and seeing my lather-covered hands. All I need to do amid the haste of the day is concentrate on these delicious physical sensations, in the moment. I can contemplate the miracle of life while standing at the basin. It's not only about the fact that afterwards I will have clean hands, but also about giving the activity my full attention and taking the time to enjoy it.

As well as creating pockets of peace in my day, hand washing is also a chance to polish my glasses. I can literally see more clearly afterwards. That's become my second mindful activity. The idea is to add more and more to your list until your day is punctuated by these enjoyable mindful moments. It can be useful to have several of these mindful activities to choose from, including one you can engage in without actually having to leave the room and disrupt a meeting (such as polishing your glasses or doodling), so you can select the best one for any given situation. I'm planning to add cleaning my teeth next week, which will make three and counting . . .

5 . STUFFOCATION

I'm still on a mission to sort out the house. Clearing cupboards also clears my mind and allows me to better enjoy those objects I've consciously decided to keep. The spring sunshine is unforgiving, illuminating the dusty piles of belongings that seem to be everywhere. There are redundant winter coats, boots, rugs, cushions, toys, books, sets of playing cards, lone chess pieces, jugs, jars, and, well, just stuff. I have resolved to start heeding the words of the nineteenth-century artist, designer, and writer William Morris who, in 1880, told us to keep only things that are useful or beautiful.

But it's tricky to strike a balance between keeping mementos of the past and reducing our possessions for the sake of space and calm. Finding this balance is especially hard for me, as I'm one of those people who finds it hard to throw things away. It runs in the family. My granny kept a mouse she'd caught in her freezer in case she ever got a cat. So I have a working rule: I save only what gives me joy or has some unequivocal, indelible link to my family or friends—this is not stuff but the stuff of dreams. These objects may not be useful but they are certainly beautiful to me. If in doubt, I imagine how mortified I would be if others found out

that something they'd given me had been chucked out.
Anything else can be thanked and sent on its way.

6. PRAYER

It's an unusually warm day for April, and I'm especially hot, as I'm wearing a thick coat. I'm also bothered—no great crisis, just a hectic day. A joy, then, to slip into the cool of our local church on my way home. Quietly praying offers me a reprieve from the rush of modern life, as well as time and space to collect my thoughts. I recite my favorite prayer, found in the breviary of Saint Teresa when she died:

> *Let nothing disturb thee,*
> *Nothing affright thee*
> *All things are passing;*
> *God never changeth;*
> *Patient endurance*
> *Attaineth to all things;*
> *Who God possesseth*
> *In nothing is wanting;*
> *Alone God sufficeth.*

These lines—so easy to learn and recite—remind me of a higher power and the fact that we are not as omniscient as sometimes we feel we are. We live in a world that tells us we should be able to solve our problems, yet many of the challenges we face are out of our control. Little is known; much is puzzling. Regardless of our personal faith, sometimes all we can do is try to develop a sense of "patient endurance" and remind ourselves that "all things are passing."

The sentiments are familiar, but the language, rhythm, and simplicity of the prayer make them seem fresh and new. I step outside, back into the sunshine. St. Teresa has brought me peace once more.

7. THREE-STEP BREATHING EXERCISE

I've just been teased by our daughter about my obsession with the importance of breathing. With an unerring grasp of biology, she reminded me that if we didn't breathe, we'd all be dead.

But athletes and singers learn to breathe, I replied. Engaging more consciously with your breath connects you to your body and helps focus your attention. How you breathe reflects how you are. Open, expansive breaths make me feel open and expansive in turn.

This particular breathing exercise is effective in helping me feel more present and comfortable in my own skin. Use it when you have a small window of time to spare and can find a quiet place to sit. Even my skeptical daughter now uses it before a demanding day. You can allow as little as a minute for each step.

Step 1

Sit down. Take note of how you feel. Try to become more aware of your body: your feet on the floor, your clothes against your skin, the beating of your heart, and the rhythm of your breath.

Notice your thoughts—just observe them with an open, nonjudgmental curiosity. Sometimes labeling them can help: "planning," "worrying." And then gently let them go, like leaves floating down a stream.

Step 2

Bring your attention inward and focus solely on your breathing. Don't feel you must change your posture, position, thoughts, or breath. Just become aware of each inhalation and exhalation, and how your body moves as you breathe.

Step 3

Expand your attention outward once more to the whole of your body. Pay attention to how your body feels, to what is on your mind, and to the space around you. At this stage you might like to turn your thoughts to others and put your own experiences into perspective. Gradually open yourself up to your surroundings and resume your day.

8. UNPLUG

The same daughter has just addressed me loudly as "Rachel." Instead of concentrating on our conversation, I've been checking my phone.

This exchange has given me fresh impetus to do something about my smartphone habit. Apparently, the average smartphone user checks their device up to nine times an hour. A third of users check their emails before 7 a.m. Some even take their smartphones to the bathroom with them. I know this to be the case because the average user is, I'm afraid, me.

The first way I've managed to reduce my habit is by recognizing its consequences. Far from making me the connected, creative person I wish to be, screens have a tendency to distract me and distance me from those I love.

My solutions are:

1. To write "Use with Caution" on my phone's bright-pink cover.

2. To try to use text and email with friends and family solely as a means of setting up face-to-face meetings.

3. To be especially vigilant about switching off my phone in the hour or so before bedtime. The artificial bright-blue light emitted by television screens, computers, and smartphones confuses our bodies. Just when we should be winding down, it tricks our brains into thinking the day is still in full swing. Our bodies can't switch off wakefulness the moment our screens go dark. There are certain apps that reduce the brightness of your screen as it gets later and later. I rely more on my aforementioned daughter to remind me that once we sit down for supper, that's a good moment to switch off my phone for the night.

9. EMBRACE THE NEW DAY

Like Snoopy, I suspect I'm allergic to mornings. But while it can be a struggle to wake up early, it's worth the effort. I've learned being a lark is better for my mental health than being an owl.

Here's what I did this morning in aid of venturing out from under my duvet:

1. I decided that there was nothing else to do but to force myself up. For me, motivation usually follows action, not the other way around.

2. I took some slow awakening breaths. Our waking thoughts can be revealing. They allow us to take the temperature of our minds and observe what has risen to the surface overnight.

3. I did some stretches. I hope one day to take up yoga, an excellent way to become more conscious of your body and its limits. But my stretches work well for now. The nearest I get to the classic yoga pose *downward dog* is when our terrier comes in and does his own stretches at the same time. Unlike me, he always greets the day with joy.

4. I opened the window and leaned out: I feel more present when I taste the weather—all the better if it's raining or windy. My mind and body seem to reunite, and I feel more harmonious.

5. I felt inspired by the quotation stuck to my bathroom mirror, copied from Max Ehrmann's "Desiderata": "You are a child of the universe, no less than the trees and the stars; you have a right to be here."

10. THINK POSITIVE

When I pick our son up from school today, the history teacher tells me that she had asked the class: "What would you need to build a pyramid?" The children were silent. Then our son piped up: "A positive attitude."

Unlike my naturally optimistic son, I've found it challenging at times to nurture my own positivity. Dark thoughts stick to my mind like Velcro, while happier ones are Teflon coated and slide away with ease. Yet just knowing this to be true has been helpful.

Working at being more attentive to good news is worth it. Some believe positivity affects everything from how quickly we recover from an operation to how long we live: the positive among us live roughly a decade longer. Others stress the *law of attraction*—we draw to us the people and events that mirror the energy that we in turn send outward. Smile, and the world smiles with you . . .

So I'm gradually retuning my at times fretful brain to be more upbeat—largely by adopting the following method. The first step is to become more aware of how negative thoughts can flood my head so swiftly that I don't always realize what's happened, other than that I've descended into a deep gloom.

Next is to realize that these thoughts aren't facts. It's worth questioning them. Many turn out to be false assumptions. If they still linger, the next step is that every time such a thought assails me, I try to welcome it and accept it by breathing it in. Then on the out breath, I see if I can find a favorable way of viewing the same event or situation. This morning, for example, I breathed in a sharp, dark sensation of fear. But as I breathed out, my positive thought was that my own experience of fear could help me connect with others who were feeling the same. I imagined the breath to be lighter and brighter. Negative thinking can become automatic, but so can positive thinking if we actively make a habit of paying more attention to the good than to the bad. Who knows, I may build a pyramid yet.

11. WORDS YOU SAY

In the pursuit of happier relationships—which determine my own happiness more than anything else—I'm trying to be more conscious of how I communicate. I always remember with embarrassment a conversation that took place one afternoon at work years ago when I was suffering from a cold and was struggling to hear properly. An outspoken colleague laughed and told me that it wasn't that I had a problem with my hearing, but with my listening. I often plot my reply while others are talking rather than concentrating on what they're saying.

I now try to say only what I need to, without overstating or understating my point, and to listen without agreeing or disagreeing. Taking more care and paying more attention to the words and phrases I use has also helped adjust my perspective.

In disagreements with others, I use phrases such as *I might be wrong, but . . .* or *You might be right, but . . .* which somehow immediately lower the tempo of the conversation and allow for a calmer, more reasonable exchange of views.

When trying to express my emotions, it also helps to say, for example, *I* feel *sad* rather than *I am sad.* I am not the feeling, nor will I always experience that emotional state—it is temporary.

And finally, I've learned to be wary of words like "never" and "always." Instead of saying "I never manage to take any exercise," it is truer to say "I didn't manage to take any exercise this week"—a reminder that tomorrow is a new day. Swapping "always" for "sometimes" also allows for the possibility of new behavior. Incidentally, this practice is equally effective when making observations about others. Telling someone that they *sometimes* fail to act with consideration, for example, rather than they *always* do, is a gentler message.

1 2 .   H A B I T   T A C K I N G

Another hot day, and I've just cycled to my favorite café, which is about a fifteen-minute ride away. Like most people, I have no trouble motivating myself to enjoy the treat of a proper coffee. But I do occasionally struggle to take sufficient exercise. Hence my appreciation for the art of habit tacking.

You choose a habit that is embedded into your schedule, like enjoying coffee, and then link a new habit to it, such as cycling. Rather than having to magically transform yourself into the kind of person who always exercises enough, you become that person by building the activity into your preexisting routine.

I like the way habit tacking works in harmony with the essence of human nature. The more inconvenient something is, the less likely we are to do it. Often we don't change not because we are inherently averse to doing things differently but because we forget or struggle to find the time.

Usually it's clear which of the things we do are in our best interests. But if in doubt, write a list of the habits that are beneficial to you and those that aren't. Luckily, force of habit also means that once you have acquired new good habits, they should stick. These can include habits about your psychological or physical health, such as how you socialize or spend your free time.

So now when I brush my teeth I have a glass of water at the same time so that I won't be dehydrated in the morning. Leaving my sneakers beside the front door encourages me to exercise more. I'm still working on tacking on some habits for healthy eating, but in the meantime I've moved the cookies to a higher shelf where someone who is five foot two can't reach them.

13. GRATITUDE

Late May, and one overcast morning, my friend and I make time for a special breakfast. We go to a local restaurant where the waiter cracks a smile and gives us a corner table. The porridge is drizzled with honey and dotted with blueberries and raisins. I feel blessed that we're together and all is well in this moment.

In the evening, I reflect on the gratitude I feel for such a pleasurable start to my day. Having suffered from depression in the past, I've found it helpful to focus on my mental *health* rather than on mental *illness*. Learning to be grateful is a key part of that philosophy.

The *Three Good Things* exercise has proved a handy tool. How it works is as follows: As you wind down for the night, think of three positive things that happened that day. Write them down in a notebook or journal. Reflect on each event, why it happened, and how you experienced it. The more detailed and specific you can be, the better.

It isn't hard to be grateful for my breakfast. Anyone would have enjoyed it. But writing about it in a detailed way makes the morning and my meal even more memorable, and saves me from taking such occasions for granted.

The second item I write down in my gratitude book is getting caught in a shower this afternoon. Because even though the letters I meant to mail got soaked, I felt an acute sense of being alive as the rain pelted down. The third item is that on returning home I thought I had lost my credit card but, to my huge relief, I found it.

Another exercise to try is one I used to do with the children when they were little. We used our fingers to remind ourselves of ten things that had happened that day that we were grateful for, but might easily have overlooked. It's an easy way to instill this habit at an early age.

SUMMER

JUNE ~ JULY ~ AUGUST

14. I WILL ARISE

Whenever I wish to escape from the dust and grime of the city, but can't, I turn to "The Lake Isle of Innisfree." William Butler Yeats's poem helps me create an imaginary haven to which I can retreat.

I will arise and go now, and go to Innisfree,
And a small cabin build there, of clay and wattles made;
Nine bean-rows will I have there, a hive for the honey-bee,
And live alone in the bee-loud glade.

And I shall have some peace there, for peace comes
    dropping slow,
Dropping from the veils of the morning to where the
    cricket sings;
There midnight's all a glimmer, and noon a purple glow,
And evening full of the linnet's wings.

I will arise and go now, for always night and day
I hear lake water lapping with low sounds by the shore;

While I stand on the roadway, or on the pavements grey,
I hear it in the deep heart's core.

The lines thrum with the sounds of animals and the

colors of plants flourishing in the sun. Yeats chronicles the delights of a full day spent in this beautifully evoked "bee-loud glade," from misty sunrise to a midnight "all a glimmer" with stars in a cloudless sky. He describes a vibrant oasis with songlike sounds, movement, and mystery to which he returns in his mind when standing "on the pavements grey." It is his little island of imagined tranquility in the midst of a bustling town; it is also mine and can be yours too.

1 5 . FLY ON THE WALL

Flies are buzzing and bumping into the windows of my study on their busy missions. I used to find these noisy bluebottles annoying, but now I'm learning to be thankful to them as they remind me to look at the world in a different way.

I've been replaying a painful conversation in my mind as I worry I may have inadvertently said an unkind thing to a friend. To get a different perspective, I'm now trying to imagine myself as a fly on the wall, observing the same conversation from a distance with calm detachment.

This different viewpoint is helping me to evaluate the exchange in a more thoughtful and less emotional way. It extends the gap between the event and my reaction to it, allowing me to be less judgmental, both of myself and of others. Perhaps my friend didn't attribute as much importance to my words as I first imagined.

When we revisualize events through our own eyes, we remain at risk of being hijacked by strong feelings. We are all prone to being self-centred or experiencing the spotlight effect, but the reality is that the people around us are far more likely to be focusing on their own thoughts and actions than on ours. In the end, I found the courage to apologize to my friend. It turned out that she had indeed not noticed anything amiss in what I had said.

It's important to be aware of the impact of our words and actions on others, and sometimes we may need to check that we have not unwittingly caused offense. But I have found it a relief to realize how little our perceived slipups occupy the thoughts of others. In my twenties and thirties, I worried intensely what people thought of me. Later, I realized that most of them weren't thinking about me at all. Now I try and focus on the truth, flawed or otherwise, of my own behavior—irrespective of what others may think or say.

16. LEARN TO LOVE THE JOURNEY

June finds me trying to feed my older offspring nourishing spinach soup as their exams are about to begin. The world will tend to judge our children on how many A and A-plus grades they achieve. The prevailing orthodoxy seems to be that we too have "succeeded" as adults if we achieve the equivalent perfect grades in our lives.

And while we all know it's supposed to be the journey that matters, I am sometimes in danger of overly focusing on the destination. Having attended a competitive school, I've had to take the time to understand that life is not a box-ticking exercise. However, I'm still prone to feeling inadequate when I define life as a series of milestones and find I'm not at the place I have decided is an arbitrary indicator of success.

I like the idea, expressed by the thirteenth-century Persian mystic Jalaluddin Rumi, that there are two kinds of intelligence: one based on learning facts and figures, and another we're born with—"A freshness in the center of the chest." We tend to put more emphasis on the first kind, but the two are equally valid.

Personally, I am at my happiest when I remember that freshness in the center of my chest, when I'm engaging in the task at hand, savoring the satisfaction of trying my best and not beating myself up if it all goes wrong. Flip into the world of results and "achievement," and I quickly become anxious, pressurized by my own and society's expectations.

So while there's no avoiding exams, and you probably shouldn't tear up your child's report, do try and tear up the one in your own head.

17. FIND EXERCISE YOU ENJOY

Back in the old days when most of us lived off the land, there was no such thing as exercise. People's very existence provided them with a daily workout. Now, like everyone else, I need to motivate myself to keep fit. I've only begun to achieve this by realizing how much more alive I feel when I live in my body as well as my mind.

I like to exercise outside, surrounded by nature. Simply stretching and looking up at the vastness of the sky somehow helps dissipate strong emotions. My thoughts seem to slide down the back of my head and evaporate into the air. They become like the clouds, to be observed as they pass by.

I've also found it rejuvenating to return to an activity I loved as a child—dancing—and reclaim a part of myself that had fallen by the wayside as I grew up. Mastering dance steps requires concentration and disbands the worries floating around my mind. The movement grounds me as I have to focus on my feet and the floor. I feel free and unforced, moving to the beat. I also turn pink and break a sweat, which I've learned is crucial to improving my mood.

Dance feels playful and spontaneous. If I go to a class, my fellow dancers are warm, supportive, and encouraging. It's therapeutic to be part of such a group. But you don't need a class: just throw on some music and dance around the kitchen table with your friends.

1 8 .   R E A C H I N G   O U T

I've been trying to fit a hammock into our back garden, partly inspired by another baking-hot day and my pleasure in spotting a cabbage-white butterfly among the nasturtiums, but mainly because I've been reading a book about the Ye'kuana tribe of Venezuela. The writer describes their idyllic world, where children and adults sit close together and rest in the same hammock. Their physical proximity and interaction is natural and unforced, and their babies benefit from being continuously carried by their mothers till they can crawl.

As babies, touch is the first sense we develop in the womb. Infants are programmed to seek out warmth: we need to stay close to our parents in order to survive. Yet, as we grow up, we move into a world in which everyday physical contact is minimized.

For many, this results in the loss of tender touch and all its calming benefits. Teachers and nurses are now advised to be wary of touching those in their care, and many of them lament that this is the case. So often, all it would take to reassure a troubled student or patient would be a warm embrace. Even a brief hug releases a whoosh of soothing oxytocin, reducing stress and stimulating the brain's reward circuit.

Next time you hug someone, notice the difference when you hold them for that little bit longer, softly acknowledging their physical presence with yours. We can't all move to the rain forest, but maybe such gestures will take us halfway there.

19. BALM OF HURT MINDS

The summer holidays are here and I should, in theory, sleep more soundly, since I no longer have to fret about the car pool. But unfortunately, sleeplessness can be a challenge. And it seems to get worse when the days become longer and lighter. I crave the deep, oblivious sleep that Shakespeare called "the balm of hurt minds."

I've taken a step toward defeating my insomnia by recognizing that getting enough sleep is not the main issue. In fact, it's worrying about not getting off to sleep that is bad for my health. If the worrying starts, I find it reassuring to realize that my body is cleverer than my mind. When I am truly tired, I will drop off and get the sleep I need. I don't have to do anything except trust that when I'm tired enough, sleep will come. And that's the paradox: to achieve sleep, I have to abandon the imperative to achieve it.

I also believe in taking more practical steps toward what doctors now call good *sleep hygiene*. Many of you may know these tips already:

- Snacking on an oatcake: this will keep your blood sugar more balanced overnight and help your body produce the sleep hormone melatonin

- A wind-down routine that excludes anything too stimulating
- A regular bedtime
- A completely dark room

Sometimes, despite all these efforts, I still find it hard to nod off. I've found that learning or reciting a poem can help, and I have a pile of poetry books by my bedside in case. I've just been learning "A Boy's Song" by James Hogg with its hypnotic lines: "Where the pools are bright and deep/Where the grey trout lies asleep." Here's hoping that with the right preparation and a kind attitude toward yourself, you'll receive the balm of a good night's rest.

20. FLOWER POWER

It's the time of year that finds me in our small back garden, drinking in the hot reds and yellows of the dahlias and marigolds, delighting in the sound of the bees buzzing and the splash of the hose, swigging a cup of mud-flecked tea. This is the sort of day that warms my soul and gets me humming the tune to "Walking on Sunshine" and agreeing that it does indeed feel good.

It might seem obvious to us gardeners that going green can help beat the blues. Today, before retreating outside, I felt overwhelmed by all the moving parts in my life: the chaos of trying to work on a temperamental computer and organize and entertain the children who are still on holiday. But deadheading the roses and picking out the faded sweet peas has given me a sense of regaining control.

Gardening also reminds me that "this too shall pass," because nowhere is this idea more evident than in a garden—a living monument to the healing passage of time. Believe it or not, there is also a bacterium in soil that has been found to boost levels of serotonin, the hormone responsible for regulating mood.

Humankind has long known the value of gardening. Court physicians in ancient Egypt prescribed garden walks for the mentally unwell; the Roman satirist Juvenal exhorted us to "live as a lover of the hoe and master of the vegetable patch"; and more recently gardening has been used as therapy for war veterans with post-traumatic stress disorder.

For those days when I don't have enough time to be in my own garden, the following practice is a good shortcut. Find a fragrant flower as you are walking along—any will do. Hold it under your nose, close your eyes, take three or four breaths, and inhale deeply. I find it impossible not to walk on with a spring in my step and my head held up a little higher.

21. IF YOU CAN KEEP YOUR HEAD

Recently we traveled to Spain on holiday. My favorite bag was stolen the day after we arrived, confirming my view that often holidays can be deeply stressful—at least partly because of the pressure to be relaxed. Our daughter glimpsed a dark-haired woman in the bathroom and greeted her with a cheery "¡Hola!" The shadowy figure quickly disappeared, taking with her the bag, which held all the essentials of a life that functions, including passports, cash, phone, and keys.

Everyone blamed everyone else and we were all tense and unnerved, harboring the irrational fear that the thief or thieves might return. My own way of staying calm in the crisis was to revisit "If" by Rudyard Kipling. Its opening verse will be familiar to many, but like all good poetry it spoke to me in a new way that day.

If you can keep your head when all about you
Are losing theirs and blaming it on you,
If you can trust yourself when all men doubt you,
But make allowance for their doubting too . . .

These lines reminded me of the importance of staying

steady and not joining in with the general sense of alarm. It was just the loss of a bag. There was no need to be a drama queen and, thanks to Kipling, I wasn't (for long).

Like millions of others, I often turn to "If" when in need of solace and guidance. I quote the final verse here, as it's impossible to improve on Kipling's own words.

If you can talk with crowds and keep your virtue,
Or walk with Kings—nor lose the common touch,
If neither foes nor loving friends can hurt you,
If all men count with you, but none too much;
If you can fill the unforgiving minute
With sixty seconds' worth of distance run,
Yours is the Earth and everything that's in it,
And—which is more—you'll be a Man, my son!

22. NOURISH YOUR BODY

After my bag was stolen on our summer holidays, I took awhile to fully relax, far from home in the hot Spanish night. There's a saying, however, that it is only when our hands are emptied that we can receive something new. And so it proved in this instance.

The lady who lived next door to our holiday home turned out to be a nutritionist and a wonderfully wise and kind person. She provided a bottle of *pastillas* (pills) to help me regain that holiday feeling as well as a basket of homegrown tomatoes, warm from the pots on her balcony and sweetly scented.

The tablets turned out to be vitamin B supplements. She reminded me that low mood is often associated with vitamin B deficiency. In the past I had taken supplements, but had forgotten to do so for the last few months. Thanks to her, I restarted taking the vitamins B_3, B_6, and B_{12} twice a day. The effect was instantaneous, dramatic, and helped me enjoy the rest of the holiday.

Back home, I now take my B vitamins religiously and notice a difference when I don't. Just as important was my delight in how a stranger exemplified the sort of kindness that cheers the spirit.

23. THE SOUND OF RUNNING WATER

Today is the kind of hot, dusty August day that begs me to visit the Japanese garden in our local park. Enclosed within the grounds, the garden abounds with carefully pruned maples and shrubs set between smooth, round rocks and mounds of bright-green moss. At its heart is a waterfall that flows into a pond of giant carp.

I sit down on one of the large slabs of sun-warmed stone in front of the waterfall. The other visitors and tourists, laughing and shouting, begin to fade from my consciousness as I close my eyes and listen to the water for three or four minutes.

Each second is accompanied by the splashing water hitting the smooth surface of the pond. The drops are like pearls on a necklace, falling in an orderly way, one at a time. When I get up, I feel rejuvenated. My head has emptied of its worries, almost as if they have flowed into the water.

I'm not quite sure why running water is so calming. Maybe it's the perpetual motion: it never ceases to move and is full of vitality. Maybe it's the soothing sound that muffles the loud noises of a big city, giving us a sense of peace. Maybe it's the realization that something as hard as rock can be worn away by something as soft as water. Or perhaps it's because humans are 70 percent water, and somehow we are reminded of the connection between the water within us and the water without. Become separate from nature, and we become separate from ourselves.

24. THE JOY OF MISSING OUT

I hate missing out, and today is no exception. I've got a bad headache and can't join a friend's surprise birthday celebrations. For me, FOMO—or the *Fear of Missing Out*—can be a problem. But one insight has allowed me to change my outlook and become someone who can become a JOMO (*Joy of Missing Out*) type, at least some of the time.

The secret is this: even if I did manage to accept every invitation, never miss any event, or finally complete that wretched to-do list—I'd still be missing out: on the serenity and freedom of doing nothing. It's known as *the opportunity cost*. Whatever path you choose, an option has been forgone. So instead of fretting about missing the party, I can learn to savor lying in bed with a hot water bottle and my detective novel. That too is an important and valid way of spending my time.

Should I need any further motivation, there are important biological reasons to beware of becoming a FOMO type. I've learned that if I fail to stop, and remain high on a cocktail of busyness and stress hormones, one day I'm in danger of simply collapsing. I know this as I've done exactly that in the past. Sometimes I find it helpful to imagine that being overly busy is like racing down a dangerous alleyway. Exhilarating at first, but continue for too long, and eventually a sniper will hit you.

I've also gradually become aware that a constant need to emphasize a packed schedule can be related to insecurity. We value the idea of being a busy person. But the truly confident, I notice, tend not to measure their lives by how many events they attend. Rather, they seem to enjoy a quiet inner contentment.

25. MENDING

I'm often at my most serene when mending, whether it's stitching a button back on a shirt or managing to reattach the arm to my broken glasses with a tiny paperclip that is serving as a missing screw.

Today I'm piecing together a flower-patterned vase, which I knocked off the kitchen table. Thanks to a happy half hour with my superglue, the vase is whole once more, though it's easy to spot the spidery breaks and the gobbets of hardened glue.

The process reminds me of what happens in Japan when a treasured piece of pottery gets broken. Practitioners of an art known as *kintsugi,* or *golden joinery,* mix their glue with powdered gold to deliberately make a feature of the repaired cracks. The piece thereby becomes unique, and arguably more beautiful.

I feel as if I too have undergone this repair process. Like a broken Japanese pot, I have experienced cracks and breaks, but time and patience have helped put me back together again. I'm sometimes asked if I would rather never have suffered from depression. Of course I would rather not have been unwell, but I also recognize it has made me who I am, not least the person who is delighted to be well. Like the cracks on a Japanese pot, it's part of me and my history, not something I'm trying to disguise.

It's an idea that makes me as calm as the time spent mending does. And my glasses are still intact.

26. HOME CALMER HOME

I love buying flowers. And this week was no different. I couldn't resist the arrangements in their pale-blue tin buckets. I bought a small bunch of purple peonies, so perfect they look as if they're made of porcelain.

We spend on average eight hours a day at home, yet psychologists have found that many of us don't find our house or apartment restful. I'm someone who's happier outdoors—so I use flowers on special occasions and plants more routinely to bring some of that feeling into our house.

Another strategy for creating a calm interior could be to fill your home with colorful pictures. It has been shown that office workers who visit an art gallery during their lunch breaks record lower stress levels.

In my own home, our fridge is covered in a patchwork of postcards and torn-out humorous articles that cheer me up. Similarly, I find that photos of family and friends help rescue me from obsessing about my own concerns and evoke treasured memories. Faded old photos of ancient relatives are especially helpful. They give me a sense of the passing generations, which puts things in perspective and makes me feel part of the bigger picture.

AUTUMN

SEPTEMBER ~ OCTOBER ~ NOVEMBER

27. MAKE ME THY LYRE

Here's an excerpt from Percy Bysshe Shelley's "Ode to the West Wind." I love these verses for giving me a sense of hope and an appreciation of the "mighty harmonies" of autumn, as the end of summer can make me feel melancholic.

Make me thy lyre, even as the forest is:
What if my leaves are falling like its own!
The tumult of thy mighty harmonies

Will take from both a deep, autumnal tone,
Sweet though in sadness. Be thou, Spirit fierce,
My spirit! Be thou me, impetuous one!

Drive my dead thoughts over the universe
Like withered leaves to quicken a new birth!
And, by the incantation of this verse,

Scatter, as from an unextinguished hearth
Ashes and sparks, my words among mankind!
Be through my lips to unawakened earth

The trumpet of a prophecy! O Wind,
If Winter comes, can Spring be far behind?

The description of an "autumnal tone" that is "sweet though in sadness" sums up the sometimes ambivalent feelings brought on by a season that marks the end of easy warmth and abundant greenery. The poem promises new growth, even when the scene seems unpromising. "Withered leaves" will enrich the soil and bring about "new birth." The "unawakened earth" is waiting to burst into life.

Autumn, we are reassured, is a necessary part of our year. It's also the start of the new school year, which brings a sense of fresh resolve and new pencil cases. And "If Winter comes," Shelley asks, "can Spring be far behind?" These are my favorite lines in the poem. We can relax and trust in the inevitability of the seasons, time's passing, and nature's wisdom. Becoming more attuned to the seasons and their rhythm may help us to find the natural rhythm in our own lives.

28. BIRD BY BIRD

A marital summit: I fear we have both taken on too much. Unlike my husband, who remains cool and collected, I'm feeling overwhelmed. I want to stop, press pause, and consider how to engage with all the tasks at hand.

The answer is to remind myself of the American author Anne Lamott, who wrote one of my favorite books on what made for a life well lived. It's called *Bird by Bird*.

In the book, she remembers her ten-year-old brother trying to write a report on birds that he'd had three months to complete and that was now due the next day. The child is close to tears at the kitchen table, surrounded by paper and pens and unopened books on ornithology, immobilized by the immensity of the task ahead. Lamott's father sits down beside his son, puts his arm around him, and says, "Bird by bird, buddy. Just take it bird by bird."

Such advice—to slow down and take life in small chunks, even minute by minute—has never felt timelier to me. Minutes come one at a time. Never in my whole life will I have to deal with more than the next sixty seconds at one time. And nor will you.

I feel much better now that I realize it is only possible to do so much in each day. I approach my life bird by bird.

29. MAKE MISTAKES

I have to decide which of two work options to pursue. It will be impossible to do both. I used to hate making choices like these; nothing would get me more rattled than the feeling that I would choose the wrong path and miss a golden opportunity. I'm learning to readjust my thinking in order to make decision making less stressful.

First I take into account what my body is saying. Sometimes my head says one thing and my body the opposite. This may mean something is not right for me, in which case I try and listen to my intuition. Sometimes, however, the ball of fear in the pit of my stomach may mean I'm close to doing something that, though frightening, is important for growth and change.

Once I've chosen a course of action, I remind myself of one of my favorite postcards with the slogan "I've made so many mistakes, and I've learned so much, I'm thinking of making some more."

Most important, I've learned that it's not the supposed mistakes that matter but how we view or respond to them. The difference between stumbling blocks and stepping stones is how we use them. One of the differences between positive and negative thinkers is how they view what we unhelpfully describe as *failure*.

Some people see it as an opportunity to try again and *fail better* next time, while others treat it as an excuse to give up.

This has helped me abandon the idea that there is any such thing as an entirely good or bad decision. Life unfolds and what happens, happens. Sometimes good ideas can have bad results, and supposedly bad ideas can lead to something good.

The inventor Thomas Edison was a marvelous example of someone unafraid of making a mistake. While trying to develop a new battery, he conducted over nine thousand experiments that failed to yield the outcome he was looking for. When asked if he was disappointed by the lack of results, he said: "Results! Why, man, I have gotten a lot of results! I know several thousand things that won't work."

I've learned not to expect success the first time around, and now that I've learned to embrace mistakes like Edison, decision making has lost its sting.

30. BOX SETS

Good news: I no longer need to feel guilty about watching my box sets of violent crime series, as I've discovered they might be an unlikely source of calm. I used to be so uneasy about my compulsive viewing habits that I once watched an entire series hidden in our bedroom cupboard.

My love of these compelling shows has long since heightened my sense of gratitude. I feel thankful that I don't have to run a crystal-meth empire and that I'm not being hunted down by a madman under melancholic Nordic skies. After each viewing session I hug the first member of the family I encounter, relishing my peaceful, law-abiding life.

But now I've learned that watching scary stories also grounds us in the present by making us more alert to our surroundings. It can even boost our sense of well-being by activating the production of dopamine and serotonin in our brains.

Some scientists liken the fear these dramatic television shows generate to riding a roller coaster: it's not always comfortable, but it's exhilarating to look back and say you did it. Controlled experiences of fear help us feel more empowered by increasing our tolerance for the unknown and unexpected while simultaneously highlighting our relative safety and contentment.

Time for another episode, and this time I'm sitting on the sofa.

31. THE ROAD BETTER TRAVELED

I have been traveling around the country a lot in the last few weeks, not something I find easy. I've had anxiety about traveling ever since I was a small child and have been known to show up two hours early to catch a train. I'm not much better once on board.

It might seem counterintuitive to pick what for me can be the most stressful part of the day as a time to unwind. But odd as it sounds, I'm learning to treat traveling as a good opportunity to practice relaxation. Sometimes it's the only part of the day I get to myself.

So yesterday, as the train pulled out of the station, I shut my eyes for a moment to focus on its rhythmic movement. I felt the velvety seat material. I noticed the slight draft coming in through the window. The calm I experienced meant I could work my way through various work reports that I had brought with me.

On arrival, I used the sound of a distant siren as a call to attention, a reminder to become more conscious of my thoughts and to focus on the here and now. While walking to my destination, instead of searching for a break in the traffic to dash across the road, I enjoyed the minute's wait at the lights. Every delay was a chance to be present rather than impatient.

Adopting these habits has helped me reduce the unease that used to assail me and has turned my journeys into something happier instead.

Despite my valiant efforts, my family still seems to avoid traveling with me if possible . . .

3 2 . FIND A COMPANION

Sammy and I are just back from a walk around the neighborhood. He is young, fit, and attractive. His eyes are staring into mine. However bad tempered I may be, he proffers nothing but love in return. He is always pleased to see me. I've never known anyone who so lives in the moment.

I wish I could learn his secrets. The only problem is he's our shaggy-haired, golden-brown terrier.

Having a dog has proved to be the perfect stress reliever. Stroking Sammy and sitting with him curled up on my lap makes my blood pressure drop and my heart rate slow down. He helps me get the mood-boosting exercise that is so essential to my sense of well-being. I love meeting all his friends and their owners too, especially if I'm feeling lonely. He even helps me when I go to the hairdresser's. When I need to remember what shade my hair needs dyeing, I show them a photo of Sammy and his perfect shade of "bronde."

Of course, you may not be able to own a pet, but perhaps you can borrow one occasionally. As much as I like to think Sammy loves me alone, he will stare adoringly into your eyes too if he thinks it's time for a walk.

33. FIND YOUR MIDPOINT

I had some positive feedback today about a project I'm working on. I'm learning, however, to try not to let achievements determine my sense of self-worth. Instead, I find I'm steadier if I stay balanced and remain at mid-point.

When things go well, it's lovely for a time. People congratulate you, wanting to know how you've pulled off some feat or other. Such attention and flattery can feel very welcome, and I don't want to sound like a killjoy: of course there's a time for celebration.

But it can also be a little unnerving if you are prone to mood swings. Was I really so dull before my luck changed? If my next project fails, will admiration turn to indifference? The problem with believing the "I'm so special" phase that follows a success is that when your luck changes, you are likely to believe just the opposite: "I'm so worthless."

In fact, neither is true. You are not more special when the world smiles on you, nor does your value diminish when things don't work out. This is your mid-point: a steadying mindset of valuing yourself and your endeavors that is neither inflated by external successes nor punctured by worldly defeat. Cherish your midpoint. Find that equanimity. Or as Rudyard Kipling puts it: "Meet with Triumph and Disaster/And treat those two impostors just the same."

34. BODY LANGUAGE

Just the thought of speaking in public used to make me feel as if my pounding heart was about to break out of my rib cage. But I can't avoid giving a short speech in a few weeks, so I recently went to a talk given by a life coach, and it left me marveling once again at the close links between body and mind.

I learned that different ways of standing or sitting can affect your hormones and nerves. So when speaking, you should stand with your "head up, arms thrown wide open, and taking up as much space as possible." Our coach explained that standing in this so-called "power position" not only makes you look calmer and more confident, but also increases levels of testosterone in your body, which boosts confidence and helps reduce levels of cortisol, the hormone associated with stress.

She taught us that in general, you should feel calmer if you stand or walk as much as you can throughout your working day, for example when on the phone. I personally love the idea of *walking meetings,* in which executives swap the boardroom for the park.

How you sit also makes a difference. Try reading this sitting upright, with your shoulders back. You should feel more in control than if you were slumped forward. Finally, just the simple act of smiling can make you feel happier. Try it and see.

35. WALLOW

Frustrating news, delivered by email. A professional group I hoped to join has turned me down, and the disappointment feels raw: all at once I'm reminded of past rejections I've experienced. I feel I'm not good enough.

At times like this, I'm particularly grateful to have begun to use a technique called *constructive wallowing* devised by Tina Gilbertson in her book of the same name. The idea is that it is beneficial to indulge unrestrainedly in feelings such as sadness or pain, despite the fact that we are averse to such emotions. Like the proverbial ostrich, many of us distract ourselves with our heads in the sand and deny that we are hurting.

In fact, these feelings will begin to dissipate more quickly if we fully immerse ourselves in them. So instead of trying to stop myself from crying, I allow myself to express what I'm feeling. Crying has the power to unify our thoughts, feelings, and physical body in a way that is cathartic and automatically grounds us in the present.

Follow these five steps for a good wallow: they form the acronym TRUTH, which makes them easy to remember. The technique provides a helpful path through the maelstrom of emotions including sadness, guilt, grief, remorse, anger, and regret.

1. Tell yourself the situation. Pinpoint what happened to make you feel this way.

2. Realize what you're feeling. Is it shame, upset, disappointment, sadness?

3. Uncover any self-criticism that you may be feeling—that your emotions are wrong or invalid, for example. A useful tip is to watch out for sentences with "should" in them.

4. Try to understand yourself.

5. Have the feeling. Allow it to take you over for a period of time, and then let it pass through you.

Today I found it helpful to recognize that I have a long pattern of seeking acceptance and approval. What seems to calm me is to acknowledge that the more I accept myself, the less likely I am to crave the praise of others.

36. UNWIND

I first learned relaxation exercises with the help of a cassette tape, which tells you how long ago it was, but there are now numerous relaxation apps and downloads on the market. Choose one with a voice you like: soon you will internalize it and no longer need the help of a tape, CD, or app.

While many other breathing exercises are about not changing your breathing, this particular exercise is about deliberately slowing your breath as a way of relaxing your whole body. I lie down, ideally in the middle of the day, and send my attention to each part of my body in turn by "breathing into it." I aim to deepen and slow each breath—sometimes placing my hands on my stomach helps me to feel which ones are shallow and which are deep.

Next I become aware of my senses—especially touch—by registering the parts of my body that are in contact with the floor or sofa. I deliberately tense and then relax my muscles. It's impossible to be mentally tense if you are physically relaxed.

Given how hard I sometimes find it to relax mentally, it's been a wonderful innovation to tackle the problem the other way around by relaxing my body first. It's a way of being anchored in the present and accepting and appreciating a body that I often deem imperfect.

If worrisome thoughts are especially persistent, I send my breath to each foot in turn, as these are the parts of my body farthest away from my thinking mind. I become aware of my big toe, my little toe, and all the toes in between: the spaces between the toes, then the tips of the toes themselves, including the toenails. After this I work my way back over the top of the foot, then focus on the instep, then the heel, and finally on the sole. If you're especially tense, there's always the other foot . . .

37. WHAT YOU RESIST PERSISTS

I've found it hard to acknowledge that I can be an angry person. My default response is to deny such feelings. Yet I know I feel indignant today because I think a colleague has wrongly taken credit for some work. Nothing so effectively destroys my sense of well-being as anger, so here's how I try to calm down.

The first step is realizing that there is nothing wrong with anger; it is a helpful sign that something needs addressing. Denying you are furious only makes it worse. What you resist persists. So these days I try instead to accept this unpleasant state, sometimes even imagining anger as a person I must talk to.

Breathing is another way to experience my anger—I breathe slowly until it subsides, and once I'm feeling calmer, I try to identify the root cause of my emotion. Very often the cause is that I feel I've been wronged and life is unfair. Well, sometimes it is, and on those occasions acceptance may be the only answer.

Taking the time to investigate and accept angry feelings can be challenging. But given the anxiousness I can expect if I fall back on my habitual response to suppress it, it's a battle I'll continue to fight.

38. THE MAGIC OF BAKING

It's the sort of gloomy November day that makes me want to snuggle indoors, play some cheesy eighties pop—music is the ultimate mood changer—and bake a cake.

This is despite the fact that:

- I'm often the only member of the family who eats them
- I know they are not good for my waistline
- We all know a sugar rush can make us jittery
- My cakes often don't rise

But it's fun to indulge from time to time, and my spirits are always lifted when I get into the flow of life by doing an activity that completely absorbs me. In this case, it's baking. Today, I'm attempting to make a coffee and walnut cake. And amazingly, for once, it rises like a dream.

I think one reason baking can be delightful is that while we often need to cook, we don't *need* to bake. We feel in control of pleasures that are literally of our own making. Second, like many of the activities I find peaceful, it reunites me with my senses. I'm reminded of this as I cream the butter and sugar together for the cake's icing, luxuriating in the physicality of it. Finally, it gives us permission to play and have fun.

Baking is bound up with love and celebration. We mark most milestones with cakes: christenings, birthdays, and weddings. I can still remember some of my childhood birthday cakes. I'm hoping my children will remember the ones I've made for them.

39. FORMATION FLYING

As the sun was setting one chilly evening this week, I saw a flock of geese in the sky, perhaps flying off to warmer climes.

Much like the peloton that cyclists ride in, the V formation that geese fly in helps to reduce the workload of each individual goose. Working as a team and taking turns at the front enables the flock to fly farther. Meanwhile, the honking noises they make are to encourage the frontrunner. If a goose becomes sick or injured and is forced to land, two other geese accompany it and stay with it until it is well enough to fly again.

The mantra of my generation was that we should be independent. But depending on one another can bring us closer together and strengthen the bonds between us. I've learned to try to embrace the support I'm offered without handing over responsibility entirely and to help others when I have the chance. Imagine if we all behaved more like geese. We could fly so much farther.

WINTER

DECEMBER ~ JANUARY ~ FEBRUARY

40. THE SKY IS LOW

Winter brings with it cold, bleak landscapes, short days, and reduced light. The last few weeks have been permanently overcast. Like many, I find that bad weather can evoke emotions to match, and I'm often at my gloomiest this time of the year. This poem by Emily Dickinson helps me accept that neither people nor nature can always be in sparkling form.

The sky is low, the clouds are mean,
A traveling flake of snow
Across a barn or through a rut
Debates if it will go.
A narrow wind complains all day
How some one treated him;
Nature, like us, is sometimes caught
Without her diadem.

Dickinson picks up on the close relationship that exists between our internal weather and the weather outside. I love the way she weaves in humorous touches amid the darkness, whether about the snowflake, debating whether it will travel "across a barn or through a rut," or the narrow wind, that "complains all day." Even in the worst of times, there are often opportunities to laugh and lighten the mood if we choose to find them.

Just as the year has its unlovely slumps, when Nature is caught without her crown or diadem, so too do we all have our darker days. Both are natural and—most important—transient.

41. HUMAN BEINGS, NOT HUMAN DOINGS

In the weeks before Christmas, many of us tend to hurry around even more than usual, and I'm no exception. This year, I'm determined not to get caught up in the festive madness and instead want to slow down and enjoy the celebrations. One thing that has helped is remembering that we are human *beings* who need time to be quiet; we must beware of becoming a human *doing*. An hour with no urgent task to complete or occasion to rush to attend can be all that we need to renew, recharge, and reflect more deeply.

Yet this has proved a challenge. Partly, it's a fear of missing out, which has deserved a section of its own earlier in this book; partly I also think I find it difficult to slow down because we live in a digital world inevitably sped up by instant communication and the ability to work twenty-four hours a day. Partly it may be due to how we understand time.

The Canadian writer Carl Honoré suggests that Eastern cultures tend to believe that time is cyclical and moves in great, unhurried circles, while in the West, we see time as more linear, a finite resource that's always draining away. Perhaps this explains why we are addicted to speedy action. Fast equals better, smarter, more successful, and more effective. Slow equals old, lazy, and unmotivated.

In an effort to slow down, I've found it much easier to say no if I don't give the reason why. I don't need to share that I've blanked out space in the diary for "being time." But it's making for a happier Christmas season this year.

42. SECRET BREATHING EXERCISE

It's a week of end-of-term plays. Ridiculous as it sounds, the sight of our offspring onstage can overpower me. There are certain occasions when it is appropriate to allow one's emotions to take over, but in this instance I want to remain a dignified spectator. Others in my family are less concerned. Despite all my entreaties for him to calm down, one particular relation keeps waving furiously to make his presence known to our embarrassed-looking eleven-year-old.

So I'm using my one-finger-on-the-nose breathing method to help me with two strong sentiments: exasperation with said relation (he knows who he is) coupled with the desire not to burst into tears of motherly pride. In this particular play, our daughter is an Egyptian dancer in *Joseph* and has never seemed lovelier in her midnight-blue costume with its gold sash.

This breathing trick is a really good way of collecting oneself in the face of strong emotions and is quicker and more discreet than the three-step breathing exercise. I've heard of people hyperventilating in the wings, but this stopped me being the first case in the audience.

Surreptitiously lift your hand to your face and press

a finger against one side of your nose. Then just breathe through the other nostril. Simple it may be, but the results can be spectacular. By halving the rate at which you breathe, you lower your blood pressure and trigger the body's relaxation response, which is the opposite of its fight-or-flight response, and enter a state of deep physical rest.

It works every time and did tonight. I stayed respectfully composed while some others around me wept—although I did allow myself to clap furiously and jump up to join the standing ovation as the curtain fell.

43. HALT . . .

Christmas usually means spending time with family and friends. While such gatherings are foremost a source of joy, tensions can run high. They're certainly running high today. Stressful moments seem to be coming thick and fast.

Which is why I'm indebted to the HALT technique, which has helped me to manage and moderate my responses. When I feel as if I'm about to make things worse with a rash reaction, I check in with myself to see if I'm Hungry, Angry, Lonely, or Tired. If I am, then I pause to tend to my physical and emotional well-being before I make myself even more stressed by doing something impulsive. Then I address each condition in turn.

If hungry, I eat a banana. It boosts my bloodstream with the twenty-five grams of glucose that my brain needs to work at its best.

Next I establish if my judgment is clouded by anger. Sometimes I'm both hungry and angry—the newly coined term is *hangry*. (I find *hanger* is also a common condition in children coming home from school or partners returning from work.) One of the clever things about the HALT technique is that it helps us to become aware of different feelings happening at the same time.

Next I need to figure out if I'm feeling lonely. If I am, I resist the urge to isolate myself and try to connect with another person. If that's not possible, I behave as if I were my own best friend. Finally, am I tired? And if so, can I pause for a rest of some kind?

I hope that taking a step back when caught in the throes of negative emotions can give you too the moment's reflection you need to take a productive step forward. *Reculer pour mieux sauter* is the French phrase for it—step back in order to leap higher.

44. PSYCHOBIOTICS

I find it impossible to get through the New Year without thinking I should go on a diet. The problem is I've been on many and kept to none. And so this year I am trying to do things differently.

Instead of concentrating on trying to lose weight, I've decided to focus on foods that make me feel balanced and crowd out the foods that play havoc with my mood—chiefly chocolate, which I'm drawn to when under stress. Eating what my GP calls *happy foods* helps cheer me up—fish, lean meat, and green leafy vegetables all come highly recommended.

As part of this new food-affecting-mood approach, I've learned to appreciate "good bacteria" and the foods that contain them. For decades, antibiotics have been used in medicine and animal farming, which has resulted in a reduction in the number of both good and bad bacteria in our bodies. More than ever, we need to increase our internal supplies of the good kind: friendly bugs that speed up our metabolism and improve our mood by producing serotonin and dopamine, both of which are conducive to calm, happy living.

Thus the birth of psychobiotics, a catchy name for the live organisms that, according to some experts, when eaten in adequate amounts can improve our mood. Ninety percent of the feel-good chemical serotonin in our bodies is found in the gastrointestinal tract. Not for nothing do we use the expression "gut feeling": our gut is connected to our emotional limbic system. Top probiotic foods include sauerkraut (a type of fermented cabbage), but I must confess I don't eat it regularly. Creamy live yogurt, however—so thick it stands up in the bowl—suits me fine. I also cheat a bit by taking a probiotic supplement. I've drawn a smiley face on the bottle to remind me that good bacteria can cheer me up.

Equally useful are prebiotics, which help feed our good gut bacteria. They include onions, leeks, artichokes, garlic, and asparagus. When my body's digestive system is functioning healthily, it's much easier for my mind to follow suit.

45. HABIT RELEASING

To reboot my sense of living consciously, I've made a New Year's resolution to shake up some of my routines. It's surprising what a difference it makes to sit in a different place from the usual or take an alternative route to work. Each week I'm taking a break from one well-established habit. Mindfulness experts call such changes *habit releasers*.

So here are some more habit releasers I've tried recently:

- I went to the cinema and only chose the film when I got there.
- I found some coloring pencils, an abandoned coloring book, and colored in a picture of a butterfly.
- I took a boxing class.
- I called someone I hadn't spoken to in years.

All four habit releasers made me feel more alive and awake to new sights and sounds.

Habit releasers stop me from living on automatic pilot, a state of mind where I give no thought to my choices but just mindlessly repeat what I've been doing for years. Although I was almost late for my meeting, it was worth it for the sake of a fresher, more joyful day.

46. ALCOHOL

All around me friends and relations are doing their best to give up alcohol. For me, however, every January is dry. As are most of the other months, since I tend not to drink at all.

Sometimes I wish I did when I see how much pleasure a glass of wine or two can bring. It's such an instinctive and habitual way to celebrate and to feel less stressed and inhibited at the end of a long day. Indeed, so much do I feel the pressure to join in that I often accept a glass, only to quietly abandon it moments later or empty its contents into a potted plant.

I've found over the years that alcohol plays havoc with my mood. When I was still a teenager, I discovered that even a single glass could cause merry chaos, partly because my small stature means that it doesn't take much to get me drunk.

Now on those rare occasions when I do drink I often wake in the middle of the night and sit bolt upright, consumed with anxiety. Alcohol is a depressant, which is why our mood can dip after drinking. After initially raising the levels of the neurotransmitters in our brains that tell us to feel happy, drinking depletes them. And so I've gradually learned to use my breathing techniques instead of a glass of wine to calm me down if I feel nervous walking into a party.

I find some of the other strategies in this book challenging to adopt at times. But for me, not drinking alcohol has proved easy. Giving up my phone habit, on the other hand . . .

47 . PLAY

A damp, gray February day at home, the sort of day when I feel the need to make our own entertainment. The children and I decide on a card game called Racing Demon, which I used to play when I was growing up.

We've had a long patch as a family of not playing games. This was not true when the children were little—we would play endless games, including our own invention called Cooking Pot. This involved catching the little piggies (the children) and popping them into the pot (the sofa), whereupon of course they escaped.

But I've rediscovered the joys of play. Whether I'm kicking a soccer ball around or playing a board game, the activity helps me savor the now. While a crucial element of living at a slower pace is learning to accept difficult feelings, just as important is savoring the light-hearted aspects of life we can miss by rushing around, dealing with "more important" matters.

Look at the calm that can envelop children when they are absorbed in a game. They are completely in the moment, with no notion of time. In this case, wisdom is being passed up as well as down the generations.

48. THE 60 PERCENT RULE

This week a friend came over for a cup of tea and sympathy after an especially tough January. She and her husband had visited a couples counselor. They had been worn down by the stresses of an unfulfilling Christmas holiday, critical in-laws, and seemingly ungrateful children.

"It's not quite ninety percent," said the wife of their marriage. "Actually, it's not really eighty percent," the husband corrected. "More like seventy percent," the wife added, "or even, dare I say it, sixty percent." "Yes, sixty percent is about right," concluded the husband. The pair turned to the therapist expectantly. "Well," she replied slowly, "sixty percent is amazing!"

Since hearing this, I've lived by the *60 percent rule*. If a friendship, work project, or relationship is 60 percent right, then I'm doing well. Perfection is an illusion, but the pursuit of it is real and can have damaging consequences. Beware too of perfectionism's close friends: an all-or-nothing approach; workaholism; fear of failure; and being overly sensitive to the judgment of others.

If the 60 percent rule helps you to call off the search for perfection, then it's hit the mark 100 percent.

49. BOTTLED SUNSHINE

I had to have a blood test this week and found out that I'm deficient in vitamin D.

Many of us in the UK do not have the optimum levels of this vitamin as we move into winter. The shorter days mean we are less exposed to the sun, which is what enables our skin to produce it. While the final jury is still out, some research suggests this can in turn lower our mood.

From roughly April to October, ten to fifteen minutes of daily exposure to the sun without sunscreen is usually enough for us to top off our vitamin D reserves. In winter, sunlight doesn't have enough UVB radiation, so we must live off our bodies' stores of the vitamin and supplement in other ways.

Of course, it's best to get the vitamins we need from food where possible. Oily fish, eggs, and some breakfast cereals all contain vitamin D_2. Sometimes, though, we need supplements to help us make up for what we're missing.

Vitamin D_3 is the form of vitamin D that is synthesised by the skin when exposed to sunlight, and I take mine as a tablet. (Consult your doctor about the optimum dosage, as you shouldn't take too much either.) At this time of year, I sometimes swallow it with a warming mug of hot chocolate as a treat in my favorite china cup. If the chocolate is dark enough, it can help boost serotonin levels too: a double dose of sunshine.

50. RAINBOW FOODS

I've been coughing continously for the past few days. Enough is enough. I'm determined to try and get better. So how do we stay at the top of our game even though it's so damp and cold outside? By remembering rainbows.

This was the wisdom I learned recently from a nutritionist who works with athletes from the Premier League. She teaches them to fill their plates with bright foods in every color of the rainbow for optimum health. The proof is on the plate: just eating steak and fries can't give you all the nutrients that you need.

The color in plants comes from phytonutrients, biologically active substances that protect them from both viruses and bacteria and may offer similar benefits to us. Conversely, "white foods" such as white bread and pasta are almost always less nutritious, as the goodness has been refined out of them. When we are stressed, a primal part of our brain thinks our body is in danger, and we are drawn to refined carbohydrates for the instant spike in energy that will help us escape or defend ourselves from predators. Remembering this has helped me slow down when I want to grab something white and sweet.

Instead, I now try to eat whatever vegetables make a

vibrant display. Last night it was beets, broccoli, carrots, and cabbage. Candy-pink rhubarb and oranges made a colourful pudding and are the perfect antidote to pewter skies and bare trees. These are the pleasures we need to survive what can seem like an endlessly gray February.

I have also been trying to eat more mindfully: consciously seeing, smelling, tasting, and feeling the food with every mouthful. I notice the brilliance of nature's packaging while unpeeling a tangerine or banana, or grating the zingy zest of a lemon.

Knock on wood—my cough is fast improving.

5 1 .   M E D I T A T I O N

Snow is falling in thin flakes, bringing a light coating of white and a brief stillness and hush to the city. It seems the perfect moment to consider meditation.

If you can spend thirty to forty minutes a day meditating, the area of the brain that helps regulate emotion grows larger. So does the part responsible for perspective, empathy, and compassion. This practice is especially helpful if you share my tendency to try and do too many things all at once, thus not properly enjoying any one of them. As the saying goes, "Sit in meditation for twenty minutes every day, unless you're too busy. Then sit for an hour."

Meditation is essential to becoming more conscious and living more mindfully, which means accepting whatever is happening in the moment. But it's something I've struggled with. I find it very uncomfortable to sit still, and when I first tried it I was unsure if I was actually meditating. That, of course, made me stressed.

The breakthrough came when I swapped the word "meditation" for "breathing," which made the activity feel less charged. Everyone can breathe. Everyone can meditate.

Now I love finding spare half hours for that window

I have renamed *breathing time*. I choose somewhere quiet and switch off my phone; then I simply accept whatever thoughts come into my mind without judgment while remaining attentive to each breath. The key point is that I am not trying to change or control any part of the experience. This is especially helpful if my mood dips. It allows me to ride out negative feelings rather than letting them grow.

It seems I have finally learned to meditate.

5 2 .   U N H I S T O R I C   A C T S

I've just thrown out the soggy abandoned magazines and old juice cartons that were cluttering up one of the children's bicycle baskets. They won't know it was me because I'm going to try not to tell them. I don't often manage to keep quiet about my tiny good deeds—last week it was trying to sort out the piles of unmatched socks—as I'm a great one for wanting credit for my actions, but when I do, I always feel more at peace. I think of them as *unhistoric acts*.

The phrase is by the novelist George Eliot and comes from one of the most famous lines in all literature at the conclusion of *Middlemarch,* when Eliot reflects on the impact her heroine Dorothea has had on the people around her, and on the value of those small—but immeasurably important—acts that may go unnoticed, but can be crucial for our well-being and that of others: "For the growing good of the world is partly dependent on unhistoric acts; and that things are not so ill with you and me as they might have been, is half owing to the number who have lived faithfully a hidden life, and rest in unvisited tombs."

While these small, quiet acts of kindness may not be

acknowledged in a worldly sense, they might mean the world to those who experience them.

CLOSING THOUGHTS: WHOSE VOICES ARE THEY ANYWAY?

In my quest to live a calmer, happier life, I've been hugely helped by the ideas of others, which is why I've dared to write this book. But something that has also helped greatly is trying to identify my own voice. As we grow up, we sometimes need to be cautious of beliefs inherited from our parents. Adhering to these ideas is natural when we're young, but can impede us as we grow older.

It can also be helpful to identify the punishing internal drumbeat of noisy opinions belonging to our friends, teachers, relatives, colleagues, and particularly our partners. The intensity of falling in love plants a new narrative into the brain.

The same can even be true of a fulfilling relationship with a supportive counselor or therapist that leaves us with a more positive narrative in our minds. While this new voice may guide us through life's challenges, it is still important to nurture and identify our own.

So the next time all those different voices in your head start to pass judgment or guide you toward your next move, try to become aware of who exactly is speaking. Give yourself the time and space to hear your own voice. For me, one obvious step is not rushing to ask the advice of those around me. I used to rely on others whenever I couldn't make a decision. I would follow their advice and then be unfairly annoyed at them if the outcome was unsatisfactory.

I try to have confidence in what works for me—even if I don't always manage to follow my own fifty-two small steps to happiness. I would love to hear what helps you walk on sunshine. Please share your thoughts @RachelKellyNet on Twitter #smallsteps2happiness or at www.rachel-kelly.net.

ACKNOWLEDGMENTS

I am grateful to all who have lent me their time, expertise, and support during the writing of this book. Special thanks go to my agent, Andrew Lownie, and the terrific team at Short Books, Aurea Carpenter and Klara Zak, as well as my friends and colleagues Sue Birkbeck, Sabrina Ceol, Sibylla Corcoran, Chloe Gale, Charlotte Harford, Joanna Harrison, Eliza Hoyer Millar, Crispin Kelly, Wendy Mandy, Dr. Paquita Marrin, Jonathan McAloon, Eliza Pakenham, Emma Russell, Amanda Waggott, and Lucien Williams.

FURTHER READING

Here are some suggestions for further reading and viewing, should you wish to find out more about some of the ideas in this book.

MINDFUL MOMENTS
Mindfulness: A Practical Guide to Finding Peace in a Frantic World, Mark Williams and Danny Penman, Piatkus, 2011.

Living in the Moment, Anna Black, Cico Books, 2014.

STUFFOCATION
Stuffocation: Living More with Less, James Wallman, Penguin, 2015.

FLY ON THE WALL
The Marshmallow Test: Understanding Self-Control and How to Master It, Walter Mischel, Little, Brown and Company, 2014.

REACHING OUT
The Continuum Concept: In Search of Happiness Lost, Jean Liedloff, Penguin, 1989.

FLOWER POWER
www.gardeningleave.org provides help for war veterans with PTSD.

HOME CALMER HOME
Happiness by Design: Finding Pleasure and Purpose in Everyday Life, Paul Dolan, Penguin, 2015.

BIRD BY BIRD
Bird by Bird: Some Instructions on Writing and Life, Anne Lamott, Anchor Books, 1980.

WALLOW
Constructive Wallowing: How to Beat Bad Feelings by Letting Yourself Have Them, Tina Gilbertson, Piatkus, 2014.

HUMAN BEINGS, NOT HUMAN DOINGS
Understanding and Healing Emotional Trauma: Conversations with Pioneering Clinicians and Researchers, Daniela F. Sieff, Routledge, 2014.

"In Praise of Slowness," by Carl Honoré, TEDGlobal Conference, 2005.

MEDITATION
"How Meditation Can Shape Our Brains," by Sara Lazar, TEDxCambridge, 2011.

UNHISTORIC ACTS
Middlemarch, George Eliot, Wordsworth Editions, 1993.

P.S. FALLING OFF THE WAGON
www.compassionatemind.co.uk.

"The Space Between Self-Esteem and Self-Compassion," by Kristin Neff, TEDxCentennialParkWomen Event, 2012.

NOTES TO SELF
SPACE FOR THOUGHTS AND JOTTINGS

NOTES

NOTES

NOTES

NOTES

NOTES

NOTES

NOTES

It may well be that you've fallen off the wagon in your own quest for happiness. You've lost your yen for Zen. Maybe you've become frustrated with meditation, or you're fed up with the HALT technique and quite simply want to scream at someone. Far from being present in the moment, you are, as a friend put it recently, in "several places at once."

When I find myself in that situation, I try not to berate myself. Sometimes I try and imagine talking to myself as if I were a child. I would talk to a child in a loving and forgiving way. Being kind and self-compassionate is just as important as becoming more aware and setting new intentions.

Keep the wagon rolling. You are good enough just as you are.